# Two Degrees to Carpool

*Discerning God's Call on Your Life*

by
Kimberly S. Goodnight

Bloomington, IN  Milton Keynes, UK

*AuthorHouse*™  
*1663 Liberty Drive, Suite 200*  
*Bloomington, IN 47403*  
*www.authorhouse.com*  
*Phone: 1-800-839-8640*

*AuthorHouse*™ *UK Ltd.*  
*500 Avebury Boulevard*  
*Central Milton Keynes, MK9 2BE*  
*www.authorhouse.co.uk*  
*Phone: 08001974150*

*All Biblical references taken from The Ryrie Study Bible*  
*New American Standard Translation. Charles Caldwell*  
*Ryrie, Th.D., Ph.D. Moody Press, Chicago.*

*© 2007 Kimberly S. Goodnight. All rights reserved.*

*No part of this book may be reproduced, stored in a retrieval system, or transmitted by any means without the written permission of the author.*

*First published by AuthorHouse 4/9/2007*

*ISBN: 978-1-4259-8643-8 (sc)*

*Library of Congress Control Number: 2006911254*

*Printed in the United States of America*  
*Bloomington, Indiana*

*This book is printed on acid-free paper.*

# Forward

In February of 1998 I sat in a hotel room in Frankfurt, Germany alone and scared and pregnant with my fourth child. My husband was in an all-day work meeting. I was jetlagged and worn, and the hours passed painfully slowly. My mind was racing with all the new experiences that I had been privy to during the last few days. I left the airport in tears worried about leaving my children, the fear of the long overseas travel, visiting schools, house hunting; not to mention the sheer confusion of a new culture and language were beginning to overwhelm me.

Robert and I knew the Lord was calling us to move to Germany. He had answered every checklist we had made with bold ink. We surrendered nervously to the call amid pleas and strong opposition from family members and friends. But there I sat—alone, scared, and isolated, unable to effectively communicate with the outside world.

Finally in my desperation I turned to my Bible. In tears I cried out to the Lord something to the effect of "Show me Lord. Help me. I don't know if I can do this. I'm so scared." With shaking hands I opened my Bible to Isaiah 41 and immediately my eyes fell on verse 10.

> "Do not fear, for I am with you; do not anxiously look about you, for I am your God. I will strengthen you, surely I will help you, surely I will uphold you with My righteous right hand."

*Whew! Wait! This can't be. God doesn't work that way.* So I read it again.

> "Do not fear, for I am with you; do not anxiously look about you, for I am your God. I will strengthen you, surely I will help you, surely I will uphold you with My righteous right hand."

Yep! I read that right! I remember looking around the room and quite frankly expecting to see Jesus Christ Himself sitting right next to me, smiling at me. Tears began to flow and a peace came over me. I couldn't wait for Robert to get back. In a matter of seconds peace had replaced fear. Hope had replaced desperation and joy had replaced angst. I read that passage over and over again, each time thanking God. He heard me in my time of need. He not only heard me but He answered me with His mighty words, His promise, and His strength. Right then and there I had a mini revival. Let me tell you, there's nothing better than a self-revival, just you and the Lord. There is no one looking, so you can go crazy. Needless to say, my whole demeanor changed. I committed this move to the Lord and the blessings came.

Dear friend, is God calling you to a change? Is He asking you to step out of what you know, what you thought, what you want? Is He telling you to trust Him with your life and circumstances even though the opposition is great? Do not fear!

God will make Himself known to you when He calls. Cry out to Him and you won't have to guess whether or not it is of Him. He will appear and make Himself personally known. You will recognize the call as God's. Whether in prayer, the word, a book, a song or friend, circumstance or tragedy, when God calls you, make no mistake; it is a personal call from the One who makes no mistakes.

Lord, I pray that my sisters and brothers will surrender to you and rest in your righteous right hand. Let them know that what you call us to do you will equip us for. We need not be anxious or fearful.

> In the all-powerful name of
> Your Son, Jesus,
> Amen.

# Surrender

"And walking by the Sea of Galilee, He saw two brothers, Simon who was called Peter, and Andrew his brother, casting a net into the sea; for they were fishermen. And He said to them, 'Follow Me, and I will make you fishers of men.' And they immediately left the nets, and followed Him."

Matthew 4:18-20

When did Peter and Andrew surrender? Immediately. What did they leave? Their nets. What faith! These two brothers heard God's call and dropped everything and followed Him. They had already come to Jesus. He was no stranger to them (John 1:35-42). They had accepted His salvation and went on about their lives. But they were tuned in to his voice. They recognized it with their hearts when He called. When God calls, if your heart is truly seeking Him you will hear. God's voice is direct and clear.

Peter and Andrew were fishermen. That was what they knew. But when they heard God's unmistakable call on their lives they immediately dropped their nets and left. So many times we hear God calling but we hesitate. We hesitate out of fear. We hesitate by holding onto our "nets." Peter and Andrew didn't do either. They left everything immediately and trusted God to take care of the rest.

Read the passage again and notice what they were doing when Jesus called. They were casting their nets. This was their profession. It is what they were trained for and it was how they lived. But God called them to change. He called them to change in the middle of the cast! These were not elderly men who were ready to retire. Peter and Andrew were in the prime of their lives. They were carrying on as they did every day. I think it is safe to say that they weren't looking for a life change that day. Yet they were open and obedient to the call.

There are those of us God blesses by letting us know very early on in life what we should be and do. I have friends who have always known that they wanted to be moms and not work outside the home, and I have friends who have always known that they would be in the military. But there are also those He calls for seasons. The important thing is to listen for His call and be obedient. Be open and ready. If He is calling you to make a change, like Peter and Andrew, drop everything and go! Run after the all-knowing Father. Trust Him to guide your every step.

Read Genesis 12:1.

What did God call Abram to do?

Read Exodus 3:1-10.

What did God call Moses to do?

Two men were living their lives and God called them to change. Just like Peter and Andrew, they obeyed, and what blessings they received!

Read Genesis 12:2-3.

What did God promise Abraham?

Read Genesis 21:22.

What resulted in Abraham's obedience?

Read Exodus 3:11-12.

What did God promise Moses?

Read Deuteronomy 28:1-2, 30:8-10.

What happens if we obey God?

When we obey God, His word tells us that blessings will come upon us. We will prosper abundantly in all that we do. He tells us that we will be overtaken with blessings. Let that sink in for a moment. As we obey, blessings pour onto us and over us to the point of overflowing. They then spill off of us and onto those around us. Our children are then blessed. Our families and friends are also blessed. Coworkers can even be blessed. Our obedience results in blessings to everyone around us. What a loving and compassionate God we have!

God tells us "For I know the plans I have for you, declares the Lord, plans for welfare and not for calamity to give you a future and a hope."

Jeremiah 29:11

So often we rely on the wrong things to give us a future and a hope. We rely on a job or prestige, our families or a move. "If I had the right house and circle of friends that would help me build my future." The problem with that rationale is that it is ours, not God's. We, as humans, tend to think temporally, but God in His infinite wisdom sees the bigger picture. He knows that we could have the biggest house on the block and still have no hope. He knows that we could get that much-wanted promotion and still have no future. He knows who we are. He knows what we need. He knows His plans. He knows that His plans for us are better than anything we can conceive for ourselves. He knows these things and He delights in giving you a future and a hope. Trust in His wisdom.

If God is calling you to a change, don't waste precious time. Trust Him. Trust that the creator of your life knows exactly what you are to do with that life. Surrender your will to His. Trust that His eternal blessings are greater than any earthly acclamations. Go, surrender, and be overtaken with blessings.

Truth: God calls us all.

# Where There's a Will....

Fill in the blanks.

> 5 "\_\_\_\_\_ in the Lord with all your \_\_\_\_\_,
> and do not lean on your own understanding.
> 6 In all your ways acknowledge Him, and He will make your paths straight."
> Proverbs 3:5-6

A soldier doesn't wave the white flag without first having a change of heart.

A couple doesn't walk the aisle without first pledging their hearts to each other. If our hearts aren't completely committed to God, then our actions won't follow suit.

> "The Lord is my strength and my shield,
> My heart trusts in Him, and I am helped."
> Psalm 28:7

> "He will not fear evil tidings; His heart is
> steadfast, trusting in the Lord."
>
> Psalm 112:7

The first step in surrendering to change is surrendering your heart. Without a heart change, a life change won't happen.

It is a hard thing to give, your heart. Nothing is more special. To give your heart is essentially to give your inner most being. When you give your heart to someone you give a piece of yourself. You open yourself to vulnerability, to hurt, and to failure. But what if by giving our hearts we opened ourselves to safety, to joy, and to success? There is no better place to be than where God wants you—no safer spot and no happier moment. We can work more hours, make more money, wash more clothes, teach more classes, volunteer more hours, but without a heart that is committed to God it is worthless.

> "For where your treasures is, there your
> heart will be also."
>
> Matthew 6:21

We can do so much for the sake of it, but if our hearts are not fully committed to what Christ wants for us, it is all in vain.

Sadly enough, it has taken twenty years for my heart to surrender to God's plan for my life. I fought it so often and still do at times, but the freedom it has given to me is such a blessing. It allows me to experience God at work firsthand. It takes the pressure off of me and puts the focus on Him. By surrendering my heart to His will I am able to follow instead of lead. I am able to rest instead of work. I am able to see glorious results instead of disastrous failures.

*Will*: it is a small word with big consequences.

The American Heritage Dictionary, Third Edition, gives the definition of will: "the mental faculty by which one deliberately chooses a course of action."

Choosing to surrender your will is a deliberate act of obedience to God.

In the familiar story of *The Little Engine That Could*, once the train decided that he was going up that hill with his own strength ("I think I can. I think I can."), he did. He made a conscious effort and a deliberate choice to get where he needed to go. The difference with us is that once we deliberately choose to go in the direction God wants us to go, the Heavenly Father and all-powerful Creator of the universe is right there leading us. He runs alongside of us and at times pushes us as He gently whispers, "I know you can. I know you can." When we surrender our heart to God's will, He never abandons us. He goes with us, empowering us and enabling us to fulfill His will for our lives.

> "Where can I go from Thy Spirit? Or where can I flee from Thy presence? If I ascend to Heaven Thou are there; if I make my bed in Sheol, behold, Thou art there. If I take the wings of the dawn, if I dwell in the remotest part of the sea, even there Thy hand will lead me, and Thy right hand will lay hold of me."
>
> Psalm 139:7-10

If God calls us to go, He will go with us. Whether you work in your home, choose another career, end a career, go on a mission trip, or a fight for a cause, whenever He calls you, His hand will take hold of you and lead you. There is nowhere you can escape His presence.

Make a deliberate choice to surrender your heart to God and then place your yoke on the broad shoulders of the all-powerful God and take rest in His strength and in His presence.

Truth: Sometimes He calls us from something.

# Availability Unleashed

Read Exodus 3:10-22, 4:1-17.

Every time I read this passage my first thought is "poor Moses." After everything he has been through, he finally seems happy. He has it all: a wife, family, home, and a job that pays the bills. Even his in-laws love him.

He has arrived. It has taken eighty years, but here he is. I am sure that as he woke up and kissed his wife and children and headed off for work he didn't expect a life-changing experience. And I am sure that he didn't wake up that day expecting to hear God's voice—from a burning bush no less—instructing him to leave all that he had worked for and go back to the very place he had so desperately run from. He was out doing his job, taking care of business, probably pretty comfortable with the way things were going.

But God had a plan. Everything Moses had experienced in his lifetime had brought him to that very bush. He was ready and God knew it. Everything he had gone through had prepared him for the task God had for him. What he lacked God would provide. What he doubted God would prove. God's timing was right but Moses backpedaled.

Five times Moses tried to tell God that he couldn't do it--that he had the wrong man—and five times God answered him with assurance and encouragement.

> "Who am I that I should go?"
> You're not anyone but I am. I will go with you. (Exodus 3:11-12)
>
> "O.K If I go who will I say sent me?"
> "Tell them I AM sent you the God of Abraham, Isaac, and Jacob"
> What better credentials do you need? (3:13-15)
>
> "But what if they don't believe me?"
> "Oh, they'll believe you, trust Me." (4:1-9)
>
> "But I can't even talk well."
> I will be your mouth. (4:10-12)
>
> "Not me, please send someone else. I really don't want to do it."
> Oh, you're going but I'll give you a support person you won't be alone. (4:13-17)

By ourselves we are inadequate but when we rely on God we are more than capable; we are victorious.

> "I can do all things through Christ who strengthens me."
>
> Philippians 4:13

God doesn't want our ability. He doesn't need it. He is God. He only wants our availability. You see, it's not about us; it's about God. We were created to worship and glorify Him, not help Him.

> "Everyone who is called by My name, and whom I have created for My glory, whom I have formed, even whom I have made."
>
> Isaiah 43:7

> And Jesus answered and said to him, "It is written, you shall worship the Lord your God and serve Him only."
>
> Luke 4:8

> "I urge you therefore, brethren, by the mercies of God, to present your bodies a living and holy sacrifice, acceptable to God, which is your spiritual service of worship."
>
> Romans 12:1

I love how J. Oswald puts it: "Moses knew that he was inadequate for the task, in fact, the excuses that Moses cites were the very reasons for God's selection of him." (The Believers Bible Commentary, page 91)

When we recognize our own weaknesses we are forced to trust God. David knew it (Psalm 18:1), Daniel knew it (Daniel 10:19), Peter knew it (1 Peter 4:11), as did many godly saints. When we trust God it brings glory to Him, and when we bring glory to God we have accomplished the very thing we were put on earth to do (Isaiah 43:7).

God is bigger than any circumstance. Be available and be blessed. Listen again to what God promises in return for our obedience.

> "Now it shall be, if you will diligently obey the Lord your God, being careful to do all His commandments which I command you today, the Lord your God will set you high above all the nations of the earth. And all the blessings shall come upon you and overtake you, if you will obey the Lord your God."
>
> Deuteronomy 28:1-2

Don't you want to be overtaken with blessings? Be available.

Truth: Sometimes God calls us to something.

# Withhold Nothing

"Behold, children are a gift of the Lord, the fruit of the womb is a reward."
                                                        Psalm 127:3

Read Genesis 22:1-18

As a mother I can think of nothing more precious than my four daughters. Everything we do as parents revolves around caring for our families. Inadvertently every decision we make effects them in some way.

It is a god-given instinct and our duty as parents to protect and provide for these precious gifts from God.

Verse 2

What did God ask Abraham to do?


Verse 3

When did Abraham go?

Verses 6-10

What did Abraham do?

Abraham didn't waste time. He rose early the next morning, took everything necessary for the sacrifice, headed out to the place where God had instructed him to go, and trusted in God's power. Notice in the last line of verse two God tells Abraham to "offer him there as a burnt offering on one of the mountains of **which I will tell you.**" God didn't give Abraham all the details, yet Abraham went anyway.

I imagine Abraham didn't have a very restful sleep that night. I'm sure his mind was racing with thoughts and questions. Did he dare tell Elizabeth? How would he answer the questions of Isaac over that three-day walk? How these questions must have torn at his heart. I imagine that each night as he lay down in the quiet, his heart cried out in pain. How heavy the knife must have gotten in his aged hand. I'm sure he wondered why God would ask him to do this. Yet he trusted Him. Even though in Abraham's eyes and in our eyes it didn't seem to make sense to offer his beloved Isaac, his only son, the one in whom his legacy was insured, he trusted God. As he looked up on that third day and saw the mount, did he stop and weep more tears? My heart weeps for him.

Read verse 5.

Who did Abraham say would return?

We can't always rely on our sight but we can always rely on God's. Abraham, not sure of what the future would hold, surrendered his beloved son to a loving God. He was faithful that God would deliver Isaac (we will worship and return to you). He surrendered the most precious possession he had to the One who had given it. As he walked to the site of sacrifice, fire and knife in hand, he trusted that in the end there would be a cause for worship. What faith!

Read verses 16-18.

What did God promise Abraham?

Who else received blessings out of Abraham's obedience?

When we obey God we are not the only ones who are blessed. Genesis 26:24 tells us that Isaac and all his descendants were blessed because of Abraham. In Galatians 3:8 Paul taught that God blessed the Gentiles because of Abraham's obedience. Today we as Christians are still reaping the benefits of Abraham's obedience to God. God doesn't overlook obedience. He rewards it a hundred times over.

Great blessings result from obedience—blessings that trickle down from generation to generation. What better legacy can we give our children than to give them over to the Lord? Trust Him for their provision and protection. Be confident that the God who calls can and will equip us to go.

Lest I overlook a most precious moment and lesson, let's look at verses 6-8.

As Abraham and Isaac walk together to the site of the sacrifice, Abraham not only continues to walk in faith but also models faith for his son. As father and son head to the site of sacrifice, Isaac mentions the fact that there is no sacrifice. Abraham, probably with all the strength he had, proclaims "God will provide" as they continue down the path. As parents, God gives us numerous opportunities to teach our children. It is usually through the difficult times that we can teach the most. Abraham's words were few but his actions spoke volumes!

Read verses 9-10 carefully.

Verse nine says, "They came to the place which God had told him." Abraham stayed the course. As difficult as it was he went the distance. That was by far the most heart-wrenching trip he had ever made. Emotionally overwrought, he not only arrived but also he continued on in faith as he built the altar, bound his son, and laid him on top. I see an aged man with trembling hands, eyes red and swollen from crying, raise his hand as he lovingly looks into his precious son's fearful face. The anguish Abraham must have felt in his heart but the love of God was stronger and gave him a glimpse of hope, even while death stared him in the face.

Do you trust God to deliver you? Do you trust Him to deliver your children, even when the road is hard? Even when it seems to make no sense? Even when your eyes are red and swollen? Even when you don't have all the details? Can you stretch out your hand and say, "Here I am, Lord"? Can you lay your most precious possessions on the altar?

But let's not stop there. Continue reading Genesis 22:11-13.

"And Abraham stretched out his hand...BUT God called out to him." God's intent was never to hurt Isaac but to grow Abraham. Don't you know Abraham wanted God to call out to him? I can hear a gasp of relief from Abraham, then sobs of joy. I wonder if Isaac heard God's voice too, or was it meant just for Abraham? The important thing is that Abraham heard God speak. Underneath his grief, underneath his fear, he heard God call his name and he responded.

My mind can't help but wonder, what if Abraham hadn't gone to the mount? What if in his grief he had stopped short? Would he have heard God's voice on another mount? I wonder. Ponder the terrifying thought.

> "Now the God of peace, who brought us up from the dead, the great Shepherd of the sheep through the blood of the eternal covenant, even Jesus our Lord, equip you in every good thing to do His will, working in us that which is pleasing in His sight, through Jesus Christ, to whom be the glory forever and ever. Amen."
>
> Hebrews 13:20-21

What a blessing we can give our children by teaching them to surrender their lives to God. We can let them see us, as parents, turn everything over to Him and trust Him with our greatest earthly treasures. We can say, "Here I am, Lord" and rise up early, travel the distance, and worship Him together.

Withhold nothing from the Lord and leave a blessed legacy.

> "We must hold on loosely to what we have otherwise it hurts when God pries our fingers loose."
>
> Corey Tin Boom

# To Give You a Future

Planning for the future can be complicated. There are many ways to plan and prepare: IRAs, 401Ks, stocks and bonds, real estate, and savings accounts, to name a few. Just meeting the day-to-day needs of our families can be tiring enough without thinking of the future. Yet we have to plan.

We want the best for our children. We want them to live better than we did. We want to be successful and be able to pass that success on to them.

So we make plans. We consult experts, study trends, or often just wing it. There are those who even gamble to try and secure their futures. The reality is we are not in control; God is. Everything we have or own on this earth is from God. It is His. He loans it to us for a time but ultimately it belongs to Him. No matter what we do, the truth is that we don't know exactly what the future holds. We don't know what we will have or won't have tomorrow. People work their entire lives trying to find financial security only to die penniless in the end. It is a painful reality. Should we plan? Sure, but only God can give us a future.

For years I tried to control my future. I went to college and received two different diplomas. I took odd jobs here and there. I volunteered countless hours. I spent most of my life trying to make a future for myself in vain because none of it was what God wanted for me. I fell privy to so many disappointments and roadblocks because I had not surrendered my future to God. I wanted to be in control. After all, that's what the world tells us: "Be the master of your destiny."

Read Proverbs 28:25 and fill in the blank.

"An arrogant man stirs up strife, but he who trusts in the Lord will _____."

Read on to verse 26 and fill in the blank.

"He who trusts in his own heart is a ____, But he who walks wisely will be _____."

For so long I was a fool, thinking I knew best. There were so many missed blessings; so many missed opportunities to bless. For so long I was so foolish, so disobedient. I got so weary from trying to live by my own strength that I just stopped trying at all. Even when I heard His call I was too fearful to follow. Fearing failure once more, I did nothing. My sight had failed me for so long I had forgotten, or perhaps I just rebelled from walking in faith. I found myself "just walking" and getting nowhere quick. Continuous disobedience and reliance on ourselves makes us tired and fearful. It stifles God's work in our lives.

"Walk by faith not by sight."
2 Corinthians 5:7

Who did God say should not enter His rest according to Hebrews 3:18?

Titus 1:16 is a sobering verse to the disobedient.

> "They profess to know God, but by their deeds they deny Him, being detestable and disobedient and worthless for any good deed."

It breaks my heart to think that in my disobedience I was detestable and worthless to God. It brings tears to my eyes to think how it must have broken my Heavenly Father's heart. He is the One who loves me so much that He gave His only Son to die for me. All I had to do was have faith—have faith that the One who created me knew what was best for me. I could have rested in His wisdom instead of tiring from my own. I could have blessed others with my obedience instead of being worthless to them. I could have heard the beautiful words: "Well done, my good and faithful servant" instead of my own failures playing over and over in my mind, if only I was obedient.

If God is calling you to a change, have faith that He will deliver you. Consult the omniscience Counselor. Meet with Him face to face. Rest in His wisdom. Take joy in His plans. He will work out every detail. He will equip you for every task. He will run beside you at every turn. It may not be easy. In fact it could very well be difficult. But take the opportunity to grow in your faith. If you don't go you won't know the joy and blessings in obedience. Give God control and you will have a future better than you can imagine. Then curl up in the arms of the Heavenly Father and be overtaken with His blessings. Be obedient and smile at the future.

Truth: Our ways are not necessarily His ways.

# Drop Your Nets

"…and they immediately left the nets."
Matthew 4:20

Let's face it, change is scary. No one really likes it. We want to be in control of everything, especially of our lives. The unknown is a place we don't want to visit, let alone stay there. So we drag our feet. We make up excuses. We put up roadblocks. Often we just refuse. If we're honest with ourselves and take a good look in the proverbial mirror, we see fear.

When Peter and Andrew heard God's call, verse 20 tells us that they **immediately** (emphasis mine) left their nets and followed Him. Jesus called from a dusty road, "Hey, Peter. Hey, Andrew. Come, follow me. Forget what you're doing. I've got something new and exciting for you. Come go this way. No, you can't see exactly where you're going but trust me. It'll be great. Drop those nets and come with me." (Translation mine).

It took a great deal of faith for Peter and Andrew to go, but they went.

See, they already knew Jesus. They had a relationship with Him. They trusted Him. So when He called they went.

They went in faith. They left their fishing nets—their livelihood—right there. They didn't roll them up and take them with them in case things didn't work out. They didn't fish one last time. They didn't fill their pockets with fish to take on the way. The Bible tells us they immediately dropped their nets and took off.

Read Matthew 6:25-34.

What is Christ telling us in these verses?

God's word is full of verses telling us not to be fearful, anxious, or worry. Verse 33 says to seek God first and foremost. When we do, everything else will fall into place.

The Greek word for worry means to be pulled in many directions. That's what fear and worry do to us. When we allow worry or fear to fill our thoughts we get sidetracked. Our view gets cloudy and we begin to wander, veering right and left, taking us out of God's will. But when we trust God and give Him the steering wheels to our lives, our trip is much smoother. He knows where He wants to take us and He knows the best route to get us there. He never gets off track.

Read Matthew 10:30-31.

What does God know about us?

Read Psalm 139:13-15.

When did God know us?

Read John 3:16.

Who did God give for us? Why?

Read Philippians 4:19.

What will God do for us?

Finally read John 10:10 and Ephesians 3:20.

What does God want us to have?

If God is calling you to do something new, you can be sure it is for your good and His glory. If He is calling you to change, you can rest in His wisdom. God is intimately involved in every detail of your life. He knows the very number of hairs on your head. He knew you before you were born and He has a plan for your life. He gave His precious son for you because He loves you. He will supply everything you need on your journey. He wants you to have life and have it abundantly. Not one thing is overlooked. You are His child. You are valuable to Him. He loves you.

> "Jesus loves the little children,
> All the children of the world.
> Red and yellow, black and white
> They are precious in His sight.
> Jesus loves the little children of the world."

Are you holding onto a net, child of God? If yes, express your fears to your Heavenly Father. He wants to hear from you. Pray, asking God to help you drop it immediately and run in His direction. He is able to do not just a little more but exceedingly more than we could ever ask or even think of. His power is great, matched only by His love for you. Trust in His power and love. Trust in His faithfulness.

> "Let us hold fast to the confession of our hope without wavering for He who promised is faithful."
>
> Hebrew 10:23

Drop your nets and let Him fill your heart.

# Lions and Tigers and Bears

Fear can grip our very souls. It can completely immobilize you to the point of non-recognition. If we allow it, fear can overtake our very lives.

Fear is one of Satan's biggest tools.

Read 2 Timothy 2:26.

Did you know that Satan has a will for your life? Just as God has a will of prosperity and hope for you, Satan, the destroyer, has a plan of destruction for you. The passage 1 Peter 5:8 tells us to "Be of sober spirit, be on alert. Your adversary, the devil, prowls about like a roaring lion, seeking someone to devour." Satan's plan is to devour you and make your life completely wasteful and ineffective for the Lord. Many times he does that with fear—fear of failure, fear of sickness, fear of poverty, fear of danger, fear of pain. It's all fear. Fear is Satan's wedge to get a foothold in our lives and pry an opening between God and us. Fear knows no boundaries. It effects young and old. It crosses economical and racial boundaries. Fear can grip our lives, if we allow it, and choke out any hope of prosperity. Fear enslaves us and causes us to focus on our own limitations instead of focusing on God's power.

As believers we need to remember that God's power to defeat Satan is extended freely and fully to us. God, the conqueror, has given His followers powerful armor to defeat the enemy.

Read Ephesians 6:10-18.

> "Put on the full armor of God, that you may be able to stand firm against the schemes of the devil" (Ephesians 6:11).

Going into battle fully armed gives you strength and courage to face the enemy. When we take up **HIS** armor (verse 13), not ours, we are able to resist evil (13), stand firm in truth and righteousness (14), have peace (15), not just dodge but extinguish attacks and increase our faith (16), and protect our thoughts from doubts. The great thing about God's armor is that one size fits all. Every piece is specifically designed for the Christian believer. No adjustments are needed, no trial period. Every piece fits perfectly. When we wear the entire armor we are fully covered. There are no weak spots. We can stand firm. Fear is a scheme of the devil, a calculated plot to defeat us in an effort to deem us useless in not only God's eyes but in our own eyes as well. When we don the armor of the Almighty God, nothing can penetrate us. Fear stands no chance.

We can't fight fear if we don't recognize it. In order to recognize it we need to know God's word and seek godly wisdom.

Read Proverbs 2:1-10.

Solomon instructs us to do eight important things to gain wisdom. He tells us to (1) receive his sayings, (2) treasure his commandments, (3) incline your ear, (4) incline your heart for understanding, (5) cry for discernment, (6) lift your voice for understanding, (7) seek wisdom, and (8) search for wisdom. These are all active verbs. They require action on our part. God doesn't tell us to sit back and meditate. He tells us to get out there and get busy finding the right answers—His answers.

What is the outcome if we follow these steps?

> "Then you will discern the fear of the Lord, and discover the knowledge of God" (Proverbs 2:5).

Oh, to have the knowledge of God! He tells us it is attainable if you know where to look. It's simple, really. God's wisdom is in God's word. But it takes time spent with Him daily to obtain it.

In order to defeat fear we have to accept what God is telling us. It is our responsibility to seek His wisdom and listen to His word. It is our duty to roll up our sleeves and dig deep into the word. Verse 4 tells us to "seek her as silver, and search for her as hidden treasures." Treasure isn't found in a day. Explorers spend hours upon hours meticulously searching for their silver and gold day in and day out. When we apply this to our time with God, we will find the riches that He has in store for us. As we walk in faith and obedience, God will guide us. It is then and only then that His wisdom and understanding begin to flow. Verse 9 says, "Then you will discern righteousness and justice and equity and every good course." If we do our part then God will answer us and give us wisdom and direction. Discernment comes from walking in the Spirit.

Not only will He instruct us but also He will be a shield for us. Verse 7 states, "He is a shield to those who walk in integrity." A shield protects us from harm or danger. With His shield of faith, Ephesians 6:16 clearly tells us that we will be able to extinguish all the flaming missiles of the evil one. It preserves our lives. If we seek Him and His ways He will protect us. If we believe His promises we have no need to fear.

Read Psalm 121.

When you lift your eyes to the Lord, the maker of both the heavens and earth, He will not allow your feet to slip. He guards you and shields you in everything you do from this time forth and forever. He never slumbers. He will protect you from evil. He will guard your soul. He watches over you in every circumstance, and forever. What a promise! We have the maker of the universe on our side! Is there anything too difficult for Thee?

Read Exodus 4:1-4. The Lord God Himself had just miraculously appeared to Moses and told him to go to Egypt. In the previous verses of chapter 3 God promises not only His presence with Moses but His miracles and provisions also. But Moses, in his fear, begins a series of objections: why he couldn't or shouldn't go to Egypt. God, with a brief demonstration of His power, then teaches us all a valuable lesson. In obedience to the Lord Moses threw his staff down and it became a hissing serpent. In an instant, the very symbol of what he was turned into the epitome of evil and sin. Notice what Moses did. He fled from it. He was fearful of it and rightfully so. Sin often comes upon us unexpectedly. It strikes, many times, without notice. Often we carry it about like a crutch, unaware of its pending danger. By releasing the rod to God, Moses saw it for what it was. Even with the best intentions our disobedience produces sin. The very rod of the shepherd, meant for protection can be transformed out of disobedience in an instant to bring harm to the same flock. But again, in obedience to God Moses overcame that same fear. He found the courage to literally grab the serpent—the very thing he had just moments before run from—by the tail and it once again in his hand became the symbol of love and protection. Thank the Lord that the things we are most fearful of can be conquered victoriously when we are obedient to God.

God is holy. As a holy God He cannot enter into anything that is not holy or righteous. Have faith and trust that God can lead you to holy ground. Run from the master of deception and the one who wants to destroy you. Run to the God of the universe and creator of life. Face your fear and failure and discover treasures of wisdom. Reach out to a future and a hope. Take off your shoes, child of God, and run to holy ground. Take sanctuary in the God who conquers all.

> "So I have come down to deliver them from the Egyptians, and to bring them up from that land to a good and spacious land, to a land flowing with milk and honey."
> Exodus 3:8

Truth: Fear chokes out hope.

# Stay the Course

When God calls you to change keep your eyes focused on Him. God does not call us only to abandon us. He is right there before you and alongside you. He will encourage and lift you up.

Read Exodus 13:21.

What did the Lord do for His people?

God went before the Israelites in a big way. He didn't just send them with a map. God provided a massive pillar of cloud by day and a huge pillar of fire by night. There was no mistaking that Jehovah Jireh was leading His people to the Holy Land.

God knows where He is sending you. He knows the way. He knows what lies ahead and is eager for you to arrive. He provides for us all along the way.

Read verses 17-18.

Not only did God know His people, he knew their weaknesses. There was a more direct route that the Israelites could have taken, but the Egyptians heavily guarded it. So

God in His sovereignty led His people in a different direction to save them from attack and thus discouragement. God could have conquered the Egyptians there in the land of the Philistines, but He had better plans for His people. Had He led them by way of the land of the Philistines they would have missed the blessed event of Mount Sinai (Exodus 19). They would have missed the most important meeting with their personal Savior and creator, the Almighty God.

Wouldn't you have loved to been there at the foot of the mountain, the smoke encircling like fire, the earth quaking beneath you, awaiting a word from God Himself, thunder and lightning flashing all around you, and then trembling at the sound of the trumpet? Oh, to have seen Moses climbing to the top to commune with God. To have seen his face as he returned, glowing from being in the presence of the one Holy God and to be given life instructions written in God's own handwriting. What a blessed event the Israelites would have missed had God not gently guided them in the better direction.

It may take time to arrive at the place that God has appointed for you, but trust Him to know the best route for you to travel. Trust Him at all the rest stops along the way. Find joy in the adventures you will encounter. Keep your eyes open for the blessed surprises along the way. Trust that He is able to deliver you.

Look at verse 21 again.

Not only did God go before them, He sent a tangible sight to lead them. This massive cloud that held the Shekinah Glory of God not only led the Israelites but also gave them relief from the burning heat of the sun. Staying under the cover that God so graciously provided gave them the ability to continue on their journey. Keeping their eyes on the cloud helped them stay focused on the God of the heavens. It was a constant reminder of who was in control and who went with them. When we follow God's will, we stay under His protection. He covers us with His love and protects us from the dangers of the world around us. He blankets us from the worldly elements that can discourage us.

As the heavenly cloud provided cool shade by day, the pillar of fire provided warmth and light in the blackness of the desert night. This amazing light enabled the Israelites to continue on their journey when they couldn't see what was on the road ahead. It kept wild animals at bay and was a constant warning to the Egyptians that God's presence was with the Israelites. It assured God's people that He was there even in the darkest of nights. Just as God sent His flaming light to give strength and confidence to a wandering multitude, He will surely do the same for you.

The psalmist David writes, "The Lord is my light and my salvation, whom shall I fear?" (Psalm 27:1) and in John 8:12 Jesus tells us, "I am the light of the world, he who follows Me shall not walk in the darkness, but shall have the light of the world." Keeping our eyes focused on the light allows us to stay on the path that God has chosen for us.

"Let your eyes look directly ahead, and let your gaze be fixed straight in front of you. Watch the path of your feet, and all your ways will be established. Do not turn to the right nor to the left; turn your foot from evil."
Proverbs 4:25-27

It is important to note that verse 22 of Exodus 13 tells us that God did not take away the pillar of cloud or the pillar of fire from before the people. God dwelt among the Israelites. He never left their side. But as we know, the Israelites wandered the desert for forty years. At times they kept their eyes fixed on God, resulting in blessings. At times they took their eyes off God, resulting in more time spent in the desert. By walking in the light and keeping our gaze on God, we can be free from the entanglement of sin that takes us out of the will of God. We can experience blessings when it seems we are in the middle of the desert. We can continue on in the heat of the day and we can relax in the dark of the night.

"Therefore, since we have so great a cloud of witnesses surrounding us, let us also lay aside every encumbrance and sin which so easily entangles us, and let us run with endurance the race that is set before us, fixing our eyes on Jesus, the author and perfecter of faith, who for the joy set before Him endured the cross, despising the shame, and has sat down at the right hand of the throne of God."

Hebrews 12:1-2

Don't look back at what you left. You'll begin to second-guess and doubt God. Focus on what lies ahead. In Philippians Paul gives us sound advice. Chapter 3 verses 13-14 states "…forgetting what lies behind and reaching forward to what lies ahead, I press toward the goal for the prize of the upward call of God in Christ Jesus." Keep pressing forward. The prize that God has for you is better than anything you left. Don't get caught up in "stuff." It will only entangle you and cause you to stumble.

Fix your eyes on the true light and stay the course.

# The Corporate View

I always knew that I wanted to be a mother. I knew that I'd marry and have the proverbial 2.2 kids and a house in the suburbs. But that was only after I climbed the corporate ladder, skipping a few rungs along the way and winding up beautifully perched atop my self-importance. Only after making my indelible high-heeled print on some unsuspecting corporate CEO (who was dazzled by my charm and taken aback by my insight and skill) and being given the penthouse office—then and only then would I focus on a family.

> "Set your mind on things above, not on the things that are on earth."
> 
> Colossians 3:2

I was saved at an early age but I never really heard or understood that God had a plan for my life other than what I envisioned. As I grew I picked what parts of walking with Christ that I wanted to follow. Placing my eyes on people instead of God left me with bitter disappointments and disillusions. With each passing year of college my focus on God and my future shifted. My life was spiraling downward. I had no real spiritual life, and as I reached graduation feelings of desperation began to replace feelings of success.

> "A lion has gone up from his thicket, and a destroyer of nations has set out; He has gone out from his place to make your land a waste. Your cities will be ruins without inhabitant."
>
> Jeremiah 4:7

Then God sent a tall, dark, handsome, very confident man into my life. He made me feel safe and loved. I knew that he would be a good provider and that he would take care of me. He was my escape from a dead-end world that I had created. Still trying to steer my own life, I turned to him to fix all the problems that I had created. We entered marriage with God on the sidelines and a lion laying in wait. Together we would conquer the world. Together we had big plans. But God had other plans.

> "Woe to the rebellious children, declares the Lord, who execute a plan, but not mine…"
>
> Isaiah 30:1

Disastrous choices and selfish ambition left us constantly redirecting our lives only to wind up in the same desolate wasteland time and time again. To the outside world we had it all but inside we were broken and empty. The things of this earth left us crying out for more. God, in His wisdom, allowed us to stampede our way across the world, letting us hold the reigns for a while, always reaching in just in time to keep us from spilling over the edge. But our gracious God, through twists and turns, brought us to a place of complete dependence on Him. Our marriage and family in shambles, we finally gave in and turned our lives over to our loving Father. He wrapped His tender arms around us, scooped us into His lap, and took the reigns out of our fumbling fingers into His almighty, very capable hands.

> "But now, O Lord, Thou are our Father,
> We are the clay, and Thou our potter; and
> all of us are the work of Thy hand."
> Isaiah 64:8

Exhausted and weary, we still had lessons to learn. Our footing slipped from the rungs many times, only to hear our Heavenly Father say, "Hold on. Persevere. My plans for you are great." Over the next few years God moved mightily in our lives. Through family, Christian friends, Christian fellowship, and godly teaching, God transformed our lives.

My high-heels slowly became tennis shoes. My designer clothes were traded for sweats stained with bleach and baby's breath. Self-importance was traded for humility, and my corporate ladder was not quite so high by worldly standards. Our 2.2 kids turned into four beautiful daughters. I do have the house in the suburbs, rarely neat and tidy and no decorator's dream, but it is filled with treasures much more precious than worldly things.

> "But lay up for yourselves treasures in heaven, where neither moth nor rust destroys, and where thieves do not break in or steal; for where your treasure is there will your heart be also."
> Matthew 6:20

My great career and purpose, I've come to realize, is raising these four precious girls. It's taken nineteen years to realize that God has blessed me by enabling me to do this. Now when I begin to struggle with what could have been, my loving Father will gently remind me of my precious calling with a "Mommy, can you come eat lunch with me at school today?" or a phone call: "Mom, I forgot my homework. Can you bring it to school?" And the look of joy on my daughters' faces when I arrive is better than any corporate view!

> "For he was looking for the city which has foundations, whose architect and builder is God."
>
> Hebrews 11:10

The best view is God's view.

# Run in Faith

Read Hebrews 11-12:2.

Have you ever watched a track-and-field relay race? The race starts and the first runner bolts out of the blocks, baton in hand. While his arms are pumping his eyes are fixed on what lies ahead. His goal is to run as fast as he can and pass the baton successfully to his partner. His partner stands ready.

As the first runner approaches, the second runner takes off with his hand extended behind him, eagerly awaiting the tap of the baton. His face is focused forward as he awaits his teammate's arrival so that he can run his leg of the race. Each leg of the race is the same: speed and focus, goal in sight.

When practiced, it is a beautiful sight. Discipline meets focus and goals are achieved. But without faith in teammates disaster results. Doubts creep in. Stumbles occur. Races are lost. Dreams are dashed.

In the forty verses of Hebrews 11 God gives us over twenty examples of the power of faith. "By faith Enoch… by faith Noah… by faith Sarah…." Each of these three accomplished miraculous feats because of faith. It is a common denominator throughout the word of God that connects so many people from so many backgrounds. Faith pleases God and God rewards those who practice it. Faith gives us the ability to continue down God's path. Faith puts God's power into motion. It is the key to receiving His promises. Faith keeps our eyes focused on the goal and gives us strength to persevere.

> "Now faith is the assurance of things hoped for, the conviction of things not seem."
> Hebrews 11:1

Faith teaches us to trust God and rely on His power. It is the assurance that He will deliver what He has promised. It gives us a holy vision of what we can't see with the godly confidence it has already happened. The familiar verse of Psalm 119:105 says, "Thy word is a lamp unto my feet, and a light to my path." God promises a light to our feet, enough light to see where we are to take our next step, not what is completely ahead of us. In doing so He is developing our faith. As we continue forward He gives us enough light to keep going in the darkness and enough coverage in the heat to continue. It is for our good. It teaches us to trust Him and not ourselves. It keeps our eyes on Him and not our circumstances. It keeps us headed in the right direction.

Faith is developed through prayer and action. Faith can't be grown any other way. In order to follow God's path you must first pray for His directions. Ask God to give you a clear vision of His will for you and your family. If I am having difficulties discerning God's will, I have learned to ask for a "big green light" and a "big red light" over the doors. I have too often taken the wrong door. I don't ever want to go through those doors again; they only lead to disappointment. Prayer is imperative when discerning God's will.

Along with prayer you must be willing and ready to take action. If we know His will yet are afraid to move, there is no faith. Likewise, when we move on without prayer our steps are haphazard and scattered. I have found that when I run on my knees my steps are much more carefully placed.

We all have dreams. Dreams are what often keep us going. Most dreams have to do with our homes and families. Close your eyes and imagine your dream house, your dream neighborhood, and your dream city. Then open your eyes and read Hebrews 11:14-16.

God has already prepared it for you! He has prepared a city just waiting for you—a city in a better country than you could ever imagine. The road of faith leads you there. It is the only road by which to enter. There is a city prepared by the very hands of God, a heavenly country just waiting your entrance. As Christians we will someday enter the glorious city of heaven, a city of the Eternal King with streets filled with gold, heavenly choirs of angels singing wonderful praises, and loved ones with arms open, lovingly waiting. But I believe that we can have a glimpse of that city here on earth as well. My husband and I have learned (not always the easy way) that the most wonderful place to be is the place where God wants you. He can take you halfway across the world, isolate you from any family and friends, and make you feel right at home. He can place you in the heart of the jungle and give you the comforts of the city. By his own hands He has prepared the perfect place for you here on earth as well as in heaven. Desire a better country. Desire the city God has prepared. Don't settle for less. Just as that runner fixes his eyes on the goal ahead of him, fix your eyes on the goal God has given you. Don't stray from it. Have faith and run the good race, having confidence in the power of God.

He has prepared a city for you.

# Don't Look Back

Once you know God's will and path for your life, move forward. Don't second-guess Him. It's easy to get caught up in the "what ifs" and doubts. When and if these doubts come, prayer is your best defense. Talk to your source of strength. Tell Him your fears and concerns. He will listen. Prayer is our direct line to the Master Planner. You don't need an appointment. Enter into His grace as soon as those fears arise and tell Him about them. Allow Him to work them through. Bring your questions and concerns to God. He is equipped to deal with them.

Remember Philippians 4:6?

"Be anxious for nothing but in everything by prayer and supplication with thanksgiving let your requests be made known to God." This is a great verse but we tend to focus only on the first part: "Be anxious for nothing." We skip right over the meat of the verse: "But in prayer and supplication let your requests be made known to God." Not being a bit anxious is hard in and of itself. When those concerns are not taken to the Lord they tend to stay and fester, causing anything from disobedience to health problems. I actually know people who think that it is wrong to ask God for anything. God tells us to come to Him with our requests, with our grief, with our pain, and with our fear (Matthew 21:22, Romans 1:10, James 5:13). When we don't tap correctly into the power of prayer we not only forfeit the benefits, we forfeit the power.

In Luke 11:9 Jesus tells us to "ask and it shall be given unto you." In John 14:13 He says, "Whatever you ask in my name, that I will do, that the Father may be glorified in the Son." And He repeats this in verse 14, "If you ask Me anything in My name I will do it." God doesn't expect or want us to live in fear and doubt. He has given us the privilege to come directly to Him and draw strength from Him. Prayer transforms God's power through you to bring glory to Him.

Another effective defense against doubt is to dwell on godly things.

> "Finally, brethren, whatever is true, whatever is right, whatever is pure, whatever is lovely, whatever is of good repute, if there is any excellence and if anything worthy of praise, let your mind dwell on these things."
>
> Philippians 4:8

In other words, think right! You can control your thoughts. When doubts and fears begin to creep in, crowd them out with what is true, honorable, right, pure, lovely, of good repute, excellent, and worthy of praise. Leave no room for anything else. Flood your mind with scripture, hymns, praise songs—whatever you have in your holy arsenal to defeat the enemy. If you invite him in, he'll make himself comfortable and stay. Smother him with holy thoughts and he'll flee far from you. When wrong thoughts pop into my head many times and I have no idea where they come from. I am so shocked that I can't think, so I just start talking to God about it. It generally progresses from a spontaneously made-up song to a hymn and ultimately to a praise song. But if I try to pass over these thoughts, they seem to linger and grow. Ignoring them only seems to develop them. You see, God can deliver us from sin. If we turn our thoughts over to Him immediately when they appear, He not only brings us through our sin but He delivers us to a peaceful place of beauty and blessings where we can't help but sing His praises!

With discipline and faith it is possible to receive what God has promised us. Faith overcomes all obstacles and gives us a future. Look forward in faith.

Truth: Faith in action is power.

# Mixed Messages

One of my daughters recently did a science project entitled "mixed messages." In it, she performed the Stroop Test. This test consists of a list of words of colors written in different colored inks. For example, the word *red* is written is green ink or the word *pink* may be written in black ink. You are asked to say the color of the ink that the word is written in and disregard what the word actually says. It is very confusing. Even the most astute individuals can have difficulties processing the conflicting information.

As Christians we are called to live in the world but not of the world so that we can determine the will of God (Romans 12:2). But so often we more readily accept the world's views rather than what God tells us in His word. The world sends us mixed messages and much of the time we accept them as truths. By the world's standards we are told to look out for number one, but Christ tells us to humble ourselves (Philippians 2:3). The world tells us that earthly treasures will satisfy us, but Jesus tells us that heavenly treasures sustain our souls (Luke 12:29-34). The world tells us that we are in control, but God tells us that He is in control (Jeremiah 18:6).

Mixed messages are often hard to decode, but God gave us a great tool to help. He gave us His word. The passage 1

Thessalonians 2:13 tells us that the Bible is God's message to us. It is full of His truths in which to live. Knowing God's word helps us distinguish His wisdom from the world's wisdom. In Titus Paul teaches that God's word is faithful, sound doctrine that will help us refute those who speak otherwise (Titus 1:9). Knowing God's word enables us to decode the mixed messages that are constantly being thrown at us.

When you hear God calling you to change, go to His word. Search it for answers to your questions. Ephesians 6:14 calls the Bible the belt of truth. Hebrews 4:12 tells us it is sharper than any two-edged sword, pierces as far as the division of soul and spirit, and is able to judge the thoughts and intentions of the heart. Diligently seek the word for answers and you will find what you are looking for. It is the enemy's dream for you to go into battle unprotected. What better way to defeat you than to have you virtually unprotected? Know the word of God. Wear it and use it to its full potential. Share it with your comrades and train for battle together. Don't get caught unprotected.

Mixed messages can also be discerned through prayer. Most of us view prayer as a one-way conversation. We speak, God listens, and we feel better. But that was never God's intent. Prayer is not about feelings. God desires a personal, intimate relationship with you. To have an intimate relationship there must be a two-way conversation. Thus, prayer requires that we draw up close to the Father, face to face, speaking with our hearts and listening with our lives, allowing His words to spill forth over and through us until they pierce our soul. Genuine prayer leaves no room for doubt. When we deliberately set our hearts to hear from God through prayer, we will.

The entire book of Psalms is dedicated to praise and prayer. Countless times over, David praises God for not only listening to his prayers but for answering them as well (Psalms 6:9, 34:4, 66:19-20, 99:6, 118:21, 119:26, 120:1). We are given examples throughout God's word of answered prayers in the lives of His people, from Moses to Jesus Christ Himself (John 11:41-44, Matthew 26:36-44). If Jesus Christ, the very Son of God, needed to spend time in prayer, how much more do we?

> "And they looked to Him and were radiant, and their faces shall never be ashamed."
>
> Psalm 34:5

Spending time with your Heavenly Father is life changing. His wisdom and love transform you. When seeking answers, get alone with your Heavenly Father. When needing comfort and strength, curl up in His lap. Let Him take your face in His loving hands. Tell Him your fears and needs. Then intently listen to His unfailing wisdom. Feel the Breath of Life on your face as He speaks intimately with you. Let His will become yours. Look to Him and be radiant. Then open your eyes and heart and listen.

> "I waited patiently for the Lord; and He inclined to me, and heard my cry. He brought me out of the pit of destruction, out of the miry clay; and set my feet upon a rock making my footsteps firm. And He put a new song in my mouth, a song of praise to our God."
>
> Psalm 40:1-3

Truth: Time alone with God will noticeably change your life.

# Be Careful Where Your Counsel Comes

> "Do not be wise in your own eyes, fear the Lord and turn away from evil. It will be healing to your body, and refreshment to your bones."
>
> Proverbs 3:7-8

Everywhere you turn someone wants to give you advice whether you ask for it or not. The market is flooded with self-help books and television shows. Everyone has an opinion. The problem is that opinions are subjective. They are usually based on personal background more than knowledge or truth. They are personal beliefs held true by individuals.

> "How blessed is the man who does not walk in the counsel of the wicked, nor stand in the path of the sinners, nor sit in the seat of the scoffers! But his delight is in the law of the Lord, and in His Law he meditates day and night. And he will be like a tree

> firmly planted by streams of water, which yield its fruit in its season, and its leaf does not wither; and in whatever he does, he prospers."
>
> Psalm 1:1-3

It is human nature to tend to make friends with others who possess our same beliefs and views. We are attracted to individuals and groups that will sympathize most with us. We want to be told we are right or comforted with kind words. This is not always what we need or what is best for us.

> "A wise man will hear and increase in learning, and a man of understanding will acquire wise counsel."
>
> Proverbs 1:5

As Christians we have so much wise counsel available to us through the Bible. The books of Psalms and Proverbs are full of sage advice from our Lord that has stood the test of time. God has blessed us through Christian authors and speakers, godly preachers and counselors. God encourages us to seek wise counsel and He has made it easily available to us.

> "So then do not be foolish, but understand what the will of the Lord is."
>
> Ephesians 5:17

David and Solomon both knew the importance of seeking wise counsel. I think it is no coincidence that God appropriately placed this important principle in the first chapters of both books. Likewise, the consequences of foolishness are stressed over and over again. "Fools despise wisdom and instruction" (Proverbs 1:7). "Leave the presence of a fool or you will not discern knowledge" (Proverbs 14:7). "Words from the mouth of a wise man are gracious, while the lips of a fool consume him; the beginning of his talking is folly, and the end of it is wicked madness" (Ecclesiastes 10:12-13). Foolishness always begets disaster.

Wise counsel can come from a variety of sources: godly friends and neighbors, pastoral counsel, Christian authors, and of course God's word. When God calls you to change, be careful from whom and from where you seek counsel. If you were having problems in your marriage, the best person to seek advice from is not going to be that friend who is unhappy in his or her marriage. Likewise, if God is calling you to move away from your family, your parents may not be the best council for you in deciding God's will. Each party will bring his or her personal background and feelings into the situation. It is very difficult if you are emotionally invested to give objective counsel. Seek godly counsel. Turn to God's word first and foremost. In seeking earthly advice, look to those that you know who have a deep personal relationship with the Lord.

In Psalm 32:8 David's words are encouraging. "I will instruct you and teach you in the way which you should go; I will counsel you with My eye upon you." It is a beautiful picture of one who has experienced godly wisdom and now stands eagerly ready to instruct others based on his own experiences. God gives each one of us experiences in order to grow us and to help others. Seek out those who have been where you are headed and have gloriously made it through.

Wise counsel is available. It stands the tests of time. Psalm 33:11 states, "The counsel of the Lord stands forever. The plans of His heart from generation to generation." Proverbs 3:14-15 tells us wisdom is more profitable than silver and fine gold, and that nothing you desire compares to her. Verse 17 tells us "all her paths are peace" and verse 18 tells us "she is the tree of life to those who take hold of her, and happy are all who hold her fast." Be prudent in the counsel you seek, for wise counsel is a major key to discerning the will of God. It should be taken very seriously.

> "Ah Lord God! Behold, Thou hast made the heavens and the earth by Thy great power and by Thine outstretched arm! Nothing is too difficult for Thee, who showest loving kindness to thousands, but repayest the iniquity of fathers into the bosom of their children after them, O great and mighty God. The Lord of hosts is His name; great in counsel and mighty in deed, whose eyes are open to all the ways of the sons of men, giving to everyone according to his ways and according to the fruit of his deeds."
> Jeremiah 32:17-19

Truth: Godly counsel will always lead you to God's will.

# Seek God

Seek God for wisdom. Throughout His unfailing word God comforts us with His ever-present existence. From the beginning (Genesis 1:1) He was. On earth (Psalm 84:2) He lives. For eternity (Revelation 19:6) He will reign. He is the one constant in our lives that we can trust; the one who always wants the best for us. The very name that He chose for His son, Jesus, Emmanuel, means "God with us." It is a loving reminder to all humanity that the one true God cares so much for us that He sent His one and only son as God incarnate, to live and dwell personally among us. It is His precious invitation to us to share in an intimate relationship with our everlasting Father.

Relationships require effort and time. They require a deliberate decision to seek to know someone. They are cultivated and grown. They form out of time spent together. If you want to know God, seek Him and spend time with Him alone. He desires to know you deeply. He is not in hiding. He is there waiting on you to come to Him.

> "And you will seek Me and find Me, when you search for Me with all your heart."
> Jeremiah 29:13

When faced with choices, seek God. Seek Him for wisdom. Look for Him in situations. Listen to Him for answers. Earnestly and deliberately seek God and He will guide you.

# Seek Him for His wisdom.

Why is it that as Christians we know in our hearts that the wisdom of God is infallible? Yet as humans we so often rely on our own fallible wisdom. Our human nature wrestles for control. Time and time again we are let down and disappointed. Over and over again we fail because we have relied on our own wisdom and selfish desires.

> "He who separates himself seeks his own desire, he quarrels against all sound wisdom."
>
> Proverbs 18:1

Just as Solomon asked God for wisdom (1 Kings 3:2-15), we are to ask God for wisdom. Not only do we need to ask for wisdom once, we are to ask continually in all we do. Even after God answered Solomon, granting him wisdom, Solomon repeated his requests (2 Chronicles 1:10) and continually stressed the importance of seeking godly wisdom. Proverbs was written to stress the importance of attaining and following godly wisdom, not human wisdom.

> "To know wisdom and instruction…"
>
> Proverbs 1:2

> "Make you ear attentive to wisdom…"
>
> Proverbs 2:2

> "If you seek her as silver, and search for her as hidden treasures, then you will discern the fear of the Lord, and discover the knowledge of God."
>
> Proverbs 2:4

Wisdom is acquired by knowing God and by knowing His word. The deeper we dig into God's word, the more treasures we will find. Look back at verse 4 of Proverbs 2. Solomon tells us to "search for her (wisdom) as for hidden treasures". Proverbs 3:13 states, "How blessed is the man who finds wisdom." To acquire wisdom for our lives we must search for it as if we are searching for treasures. We must devote ourselves fully to acquiring it. Wisdom is there for the taking. Whoever finds it finds riches untold. Whoever obtains wisdom is called blessed.

God is here for us. His word tells us He will help us. "Surely I will help you" (Isaiah 41:10). Our help comes from His wisdom.

> "Acquire wisdom. Acquire understanding."
>
> Proverbs 4:5

> "For wisdom is protection just as money is protection. But the advantage of knowledge is that wisdom preserves the lives of its possessors."
>
> Ecclesiastes 7:12

Dig into God's word and you'll find God's wisdom, understanding, and help.

> "But if any of you lacks wisdom, let him ask of God, who gives to all men generously and without reproach, and it will be given to him. But let him ask in faith without any doubting, for the one who doubts is like the surf of the sea driven and tossed by the wind."
>
> James 1:5-6

Many of us are like the surf. We get tossed back and forth in confusion because we haven't asked for wisdom. We rely on the wisdom of others. We think that God's wisdom is only for pastors or teachers. We sit in the pews of our churches longing for a nugget of wisdom every Sunday morning. We settle for a gold coin instead of the full of treasure chest because we lack the discipline to search for ourselves. God wants you to obtain His wisdom. He will equip you to dig deep. Don't get churned up and beat up in the world just because you fail to ask. Ask God for wisdom and sail peacefully to shore.

As God directs your path, remember He is **your** God. As His child, His wisdom belongs to you. It will strengthen and empower you as He leads you to His will. James 3:17-18 tells us that "the wisdom from above is pure, then peaceable, gentle, reasonable, full of mercy, and good fruits, unwavering, without hypocrisy. And the seed whose fruit is righteousness is sown in peace by those who make peace." Heavenly wisdom yields peace and good fruits.

> "A wise man is strong, and a man of knowledge increases power."
>
> Proverbs 24:5

# I Will Strengthen You

Moses could not have led the Israelites under his own strength. Pharaoh could have easily overtaken Moses had God allowed it to happen. But God loves to take the weak and through His power make us strong because then He will be glorified. After all, that is the very reason for our existence: to glorify God.

> "Everyone who is called by My name, And whom I have created for My glory, Whom I have formed, even whom I have made."
> Isaiah 43:7

When God asks you to step out in faith He will not only go with you but He will strengthen you. He will do it because He is faithful but more importantly to bring glory to His name. There are many examples throughout history of God empowering His people to perform mighty acts. From Moses to Paul, from missionaries to moms, God has given strength to stand and deliver to those who ask in His name.

The interesting element in gaining Christ's strength is that it comes through your weakness. It is when you have exhausted all human means and are weary and tired that Christ so often begins to work. It is at that point when you realize you can't continue on your own and are about to give in when Christ will take you in His loving arms and strengthen you. When you cry out to your loving Heavenly God with heart and arms open wide, He will come and fill them with His holy power. But they have to be empty in order to receive. There has to be that moment of recognition when you drop to your knees and release all your nets and pride and say, "God, I need your help. I need your strength. I can't do it on my own." God will not compete with anything or anyone. He will not let His glory be shared with anyone else.

> "I am the Lord, that is My name; I will not give my glory to another, nor My praise to graven images."
>
> Isaiah 42:8

You must come to Him in your humility and weakness with your heart turned wide open toward Him. When you do your life will never be the same. As creator of the universe, His power is unmatchable.

> "It is He who made the earth by His power, who established the world by His wisdom, and by His understanding He has stretched out the heavens."
>
> Jeremiah 10:12

> "He gives strength to the weary, and to him who lacks might He increases power."
>
> Isaiah 40:29

What a loving God! His power is there for the taking. His power is there for the weary. His power is there for the weak. His power is there for you.

Just as God gave Moses and the Israelites, David and Daniel His power to overcome difficult circumstances, He will give you His power to overcome your own obstacles. Paul boasts, "For when I am weak, then I am strong." When you rely on God rather than on yourself you gain the power and strength of the creator of the universe. You gain the understanding of the God Most High. Moses, in his own strength, was a failure as Pharaoh's son, but in God's strength he was a hero to a multitude of people. David, in his own strength, was an adulterating murderer, but in God's strength he was the conquering king of many nations. In his own strength, Samson was prideful and weak, but in God's strength he was powerfully unmatched. In our own strength we are miserably disastrous, but in His strength we are joyously triumphant.

Seek God's strength. He has promised it to you.

# Surely I Will Help You

When my children were learning to ride their bikes we would cover them in safety equipment. We would strap on their helmets and their knee and elbow pads. We would put air in their tires and make sure all the nuts and bolts were tightened. But making sure that they had all the right equipment wasn't all we did. The most crucial step in teaching them was running alongside of them as they pedaled, one hand on their backs and one hand on their bikes, encouraging them as they shook and wobbled. This gave them the confidence to try. Picking them up when they fell and putting them back on their bikes, all the while telling them to "keep going, you can do it," gave them the support to learn to ride.

That's what the Father promises. He tells us in Isaiah 41:10 that not only will He strengthen us but He will help and uphold us with His righteous right hand. Whether God sends you on a journey or gives you a task, you can have the confidence that He will do everything to get you where He intends you to be.

While reading Exodus one day I noticed this valuable truth. For six chapters God gives in vivid detail the exact dimensions that His tabernacle was to be constructed. Materials from gold, bronze, acacia wood, porpoise skins, and dyed linens to specific oils and spices were to be used. In Exodus 35 Moses instructs the people to give, as they felt led to provide for the work to be done. This was a daunting task at any level, let alone one that was performed by a bunch of wandering ex-slaves living in the middle of the wilderness. But Exodus 36:5-8 tells us that Moses had to issue a command to stop the people from bringing more material because "the material they had was sufficient and more than enough for all the work to perform it." See, God had already provided the people with what they needed and more (Exodus 12:35-36) before He had ordered the building of the tabernacle. He gave them exactly what they needed, before they needed it, to complete the task He would give them in the future. Nothing takes God by surprise. He is the master planner. He tightens every nut and screw, provides our safety nets, and makes sure we have all the right equipment, just as we do for our own children.

The psalmist David writes, "Behold God is my helper, the Lord is the sustainer of my soul" (Psalm 54:4) and "For Thou hast been my help, and in the shadow of Thy wings I sing for joy" (Psalm 63:7). David knew that in his own strength he would fail. He had experienced it on many occasions. But he also knew that with God's help anything was possible.

> "The Lord is my strength and my shield;
> my heart trusts in Him, and I am helped."
> Psalm 28:7

> "For I am the Lord your God, who upholds your right hand, who says to you, 'do not fear, I will help you.'"
>
> Isaiah 41:13

God wants you to succeed. Your success brings glory to Him. Not only will He help you (Psalm 54:4) but He has sent another to help us. Read John 14:16-17. As believers in Christ we have permanent access to the Holy Spirit. The root of the word *helper* is the Greek word *paraclete*, or *parakletos*, meaning "one called alongside to help." As believers, the Holy Spirit lives or abides in us forever (John 14:16). Jesus Christ Himself sent the Holy Spirit to us (John 16:7) in order to help us walk in His ways. It is our free gift, our extra perk if you will, for accepting Him as Savior and Lord of our lives (Acts 2:38), and in Him there is power (Romans 15:13) and fellowship (2 Corinthians 13:14). Just as loving parents hold onto our children as they wobble along learning to ride, God, our heavenly parent, holds us with His mighty righteous right hand as we wobble through life. He sends the Holy Spirit to run alongside of us, to empower and encourage us as we learn to ride in His name. His gentle words whisper in your ear, "You can do it. I will help you."

> "Whether you turn to the right or to the left, your ears will hear a voice behind you, saying 'This is the way; walk in it.'"
>
> Isaiah 30:21

Truth: He runs alongside you.

# Surely I Will Uphold You

Everyone loves the circus. I think most of us especially enjoy the trapeze artists. They seem to defy gravity. Flying through the air seems so effortless to them. We watch in amazement as they float gracefully from one swinging bar to the next, toes pointed, smiles on their faces, looking beautifully at ease.

The reason they succeed is because they practice. Day in and day out for hours on end, they practice. They prepare before they climb the rope. They do exercises to strengthen their muscles. They stretch. They prepare mentally. They practice their routine over and over again. By the time of their performance everything is in order. Their timing is perfect. They know exactly when to swing and how far and how hard to swing. They are focused on the task. They have faith in themselves, but more importantly they have faith in the one who will catch them.

There is the one distinct guy, the one who catches everyone. He usually doesn't do anything fancy. He just hangs upside down and catches people. He gets little recognition from the crowd but he is perhaps the most important member of the group. He keeps the trapeze artists from falling. By the grasps of his very capable hands they know they are safe. They trust him to catch them. He enables them to soar.

Our Savior is that guy. He is strong and he tells us "Surely (for certain, without a doubt) I will uphold you. You do your part and I won't let you fall. I've got the timing down pat. I know when to go and I will reach for you and bring you to safety. All you have to do is swing out in faith."

As Christians we have everything we need to succeed. Christ, His word, prayer, the Holy Spirit, He freely gives it all to us. Every time we are faithful in the small things our spiritual muscles grow. Every time we take a step in His name our faith increases and our timing improves. And every time we reach out to Him He catches us and delivers us to the very best place we could be. He enables us to soar to safety.

As humans we often fail. We don't put the time we should into His word or prayer. We aren't always prepared to follow His will. We are weak and unsure. In our humanity we stumble but God in His mighty, unfailing strength always catches us effortlessly when we keep our focus on Him.

> "Yet those who wait on the Lord will gain new strength, they will mount up with wings like eagles, they will run and not get tired. They will walk and not become weary."
>
> Isaiah 40:31

God is able to uphold you. Not only is He able, but He is willing and ready.

> "If I should say, 'My foot has slipped', Thy loving kindness. O Lord. Will hold me up."
>
> Psalm 94:18

> "Thou hast also given me the shield of Thy salvation, and Thy right hand upholds me; and Thy gentleness makes me great."
>
> Psalm 18:35

When we soar for Christ the spotlight goes on Him. Others recognize Him for who He is. They see His strength. He gets the glory. He wants us to succeed. He wants you to experience life to its fullest—to become like that trapeze artist, soaring and flying with precision and smiles. He will uphold you. He won't let you fall. Surely, without a doubt, He is able.

> "Now to Him who is able to do exceedingly abundant beyond all that we ask or think, according to the power that works within us."
>
> Ephesians 3:20

Are you ready to soar?

# My Hand Is Righteous

"And Thou didst find his heart faithful before Thee. And Thou didst make a covenant with him to give him the land of the Canaanite, Of the Hittite and the Amorite, of the Perizzite, the Jebusite, and the Girgashite – to give it to his descendants. And Thou hast fulfilled Thy promise, for Thou art righteous."

Nehemiah 9:8

"Now it shall be, if you will diligently obey the Lord your God, being careful to do all His commandments which I command you today, the Lord your God will set you high above all the nations of the earth. And all these blessings shall come upon you and overtake you, if you will obey the Lord your God."

Deuteronomy 28:1-2

Just as God was faithful to the descendants of Abraham and delivered them to the promised land, He will be faithful to you to deliver you to His promised land. When we trust God and follow His will for our lives, He makes a covenant with us. He promises His blessings. He promises to go with us. He promises to deliver us. Time and time again His faithfulness has been tested and proven. However, in order to have this covenant with our mighty God, first you must have a relationship with Him. You must first know Him as Lord and Savior of your life.

> "And without faith it is impossible to please Him, for he who comes to God must believe that He is, and that He is a rewarder of those who seek Him."
>
> Hebrews 11:6

When you accept Jesus Christ as Lord and Savior of your life, you flip the switch to His power for your life. It is such an easy process, really. The first step to letting God reign is to acknowledge that you are a sinner. Sin separates us from God. It blindfolds us and leaves us wandering in our own confusion. Romans 3:23 tells us "For all have sinned and fall short of the glory of God." We are all sinners.

The second step is to believe with your entire being that Jesus Christ is God's son—that He died for us is the only way to salvation (Romans 10:9-13). Verse 9-10 says, "If you confess with your mouth Jesus as Lord, and believe in your heart that God raised Him from the dead, you shall be saved. For with the heart man believes, resulting in righteousness, and with the mouth he confesses, resulting in salvation." Verse 13 states, "For whoever will call upon the name of the Lord will be saved." It is only through Him that the blindfold comes off and we can see our sin. And it is only through His righteous Son, Jesus, that we can be redeemed from that sin.

Thirdly, share your decision. Tell someone that you have decided to follow Christ. When we tell others of our decision we are then more apt to stay committed to following Him. It helps you stay on track and holds you accountable to your decision and to God. When you do these three simple steps, God's righteous covenant is automatically yours. He promises to go with you. Not only does He go with you He leads you. His covenant is sealed with His son's precious blood. Through Him there is deliverance. Through Him there is hope. Through Him there is love. Through Him there is power.

> "And He Himself bore our sins in His body on the cross, that we might die to sin and live to righteousness, for by His wounds you were healed."
>
> 1 Peter 2:24

Reach out to God and receive His righteousness.

# Stay to the Right

Read Genesis 48:1-19.

In biblical days the right side was a place of honor and privilege. As firstborn, Manasseh was entitled to Jacob's blessing of the birthright. When Jacob placed his right hand on Ephraim's head he gave the birthright to Ephraim. In Genesis 48, verse 18, Joseph, thinking his father had made a mistake, tried to correct him because of the importance of the symbolism. The placement of the right hand was not to be taken lightly. But God, who holds the future, had already spoken. Ephraim was placed at the right.

God makes a point in the last promise of Isaiah 41:10 to uphold you, but He makes it with an exclamation mark. He will uphold you with His righteous right hand, the symbol of power, prestige, and honor. Every word God ordained in the scriptures has value and this one is no exception. In the present day of broken promises, commitments, and contracts, it seems insignificant. But to God it packs power. It is His not-so-subtle reminder to us that He is the righteous, powerful God and the God of all authority, who is able to uphold us and keep His promises. Matthew 26:64 tells us that Jesus Himself sits at the right hand of the Father (Mark 14:62, Acts 2:34-35). It is where Christ rules alongside the Father, God.

> "He is the One whom God exalted to His right hand as Prince and a Savior, to grant repentance to Israel, and forgiveness of sins."
>
> Acts 5:31

As we saw in Genesis 48, the right is a place of entitlement but it is also a place of honor. When we become Christians we become joint heirs with Christ. We are adopted into the heavenly family. And thus we have the honor of calling God our Father. God gives us all the right to be called children of the Heavenly King. We are prince and princesses, if you will. We have heaven's entire kingdom at our disposal. With His right hand God upholds you. He upholds you with the authority and honor of the King. As Christians we are heirs to his throne, heirs to His authority, and heirs to His blessings. The right is a position of privilege.

> "But when the Son of Man comes in His glory, and all the angels with Him, then He will sit on His glorious throne. And all the nations will be gathered before Him; and He will separate them from one another, as the shepherd separates the sheep from the goats; and He will put the sheep on His right and the goats on His left. Then the King will say to those on His right, 'come, you who are blessed of My Father, inherit

the Kingdom prepared for you from the foundation of the world.'"

Matthew 25:31-34

By upholding you with His right hand God therefore places us on His right, in a place of honor. We are called blessed and placed in a position to inherit the Kingdom of God, the place that God Himself has prepared for us.

With His right hand God gives power.

> "For by their own sword they did not possess the land; and their own arm did not save them; but Thy right hand, and Thine arm, and the light of Thy presence, for Thou didst favor them."
>
> Psalm 44:3

God's right hand is powerful, but did you notice that not only do we have His hand but also His arm?

> "Thou hast a strong arm; Thy hand is mighty, Thy right hand is exalted."
>
> Psalm 89:13

The power of His hand is only magnified by the power of His almighty arm!

When we have God in our lives we have every part of Him. Our only limitations are with ourselves. Don't take it lightly that God will uphold you. Stay to His right and let Him cover you in authority, honor, and power. It is our birthright as children of God. He has promised it to us and He who promised is faithful.

> "I have set the LORD continually before me; because He is at my right hand, I will not be shaken."
>
> Psalm 16:8

Oh to be His sheep placed on the right!

# Growing Pains Bring Joy

> "Consider it all joy, my brethren, when you encounter various trials, knowing that the testing of your faith produces endurance. And let endurance have its perfect result that you may be perfect and complete, lacking in nothing."
>
> James 1:2-4

"Lord, I know that I am suppose to consider this a joy but I'm not there yet. Help me to get there." That was my desperate prayer one May night in 1991 about a week after having surgery to remove a benign tumor from my trigeminal nerve that had attached to my brainstem. I had lost the feeling on the right side of my face, my head was partially shaven, and my carefree youth had been stripped away. I was scared and uncertain. All I knew to do was pray. I had a two-year-old daughter, no income of my own, and a failing marriage. Not much to show for a girl who had been a Christian since the age of seven. Apparently I had not grown much spiritually. There was a time while in my teens that I experienced some growth but was too concerned with the world to let God control my life. Later as I experienced more freedoms I all but walked away from God. I had never dug deeper than the surface. I had never matured in my spiritual walk. So there I stayed, a babe, with no direction, or so I thought. While I had walked away from Him, God had never left me. He was still near waiting for me to come back to Him. He lovingly and wisely stayed close until I let go. Then my loving Father tenderly began to take over. As I look back I can see His hand all over the next two years of my life. He took me from a life of whirling, unhappy, discontented confusion to a life of healing, peace, and fullness—and yes, even joy.

Through trials God brought healing. It is good to note that these trials not only affected me but my family as well. By allowing God to work in my life blessings spilled over to those closest to me. Remember, dear one, that God never calls us to do anything that goes against His will or His word. Every trial can and should lead you and others to a closer, richer relationship with Him.

As God began to move in my life, I clung to James 1:2-6. I clung to the promise that He would be there with me, that I could endure, that I would be perfect and complete. I longed to experience joy and peace, two things that I had never truly had in my life. And as my grip loosened, His peace comforted. As my pain decreased, His joy increased. To my surprise, I endured triumphantly.

Is God calling you to a new place? Is He asking you to trust Him? Don't use an earthly rationale to decipher what is heavenly. It takes heavenly wisdom to understand a heavenly call. Heavenly wisdom comes from God. Secular wisdom would have told me to run, get out of my marriage, and start over. *After all, God doesn't want me to be unhappy, does He?* I thought. Earthly wisdom would have resulted in a broken family and more pain, anger, and perhaps poverty. Earthly wisdom brings chaos (James 3:13-16). But God's wisdom brings peace—productive peace (James 3:17-18). When God's wisdom reigns in your life, even in times of devastation and sadness there is peace (Luke 1:79). In times of uncertainty, there is peace (John 14:27). When God works, there is peace (Galatians 5:22-23).

Make a conscious effort to obtain peace. Fix your eyes upward. Focus on the goal. Put legs on your faith. Move forward and endure, eagerly awaiting the next tap of the heavenly baton. Stay focused on becoming perfect and complete. Grow in God. He promises peace.

Put legs on your faith and grow.

# Rest

Our third daughter is a spitfire. She is full of life, strong-willed, and she goes full-force all the time. Our move to Germany occurred when she was two. Wanting to see and experience all we could, we often took weekend trips to various places. We saw places too beautiful to describe. Being a creature of habit, it never failed that at eleven a.m. our beautiful blue-eyed, blonde-haired cherub would turn into an ill-tempered Tasmanian devil. She would fuss, cry, and do all she could to fight the sleep. We learned quickly to strap her into her stroller and take off walking. She would fight hard for twenty minutes and then, exhausted from the struggle, she would literally pass out. When she awoke she was a new child—happy, smiling, rested, and ready to go again.

When God calls you to change, make the decision to follow Him. Don't fight Him. When you have discerned His will for you, rest. Rest in the fact that He is God. Rest in the assurance that He knows what is best for you. Rest in His unmatchable strength. Rest in the comfort that He goes with you. Rest in the power of His righteous right hand. Rest in His peace. Just rest.

Throughout the Old Testament there are accounts of kings turning their hearts to the Lord and truly seeking Him. When they did, God gave them rest on every side.

> 2 Chronicles 14:7, 15:15
> 1 Kings 8:56
> 2 Samuel 7:11

So often we struggle and fight God's plans for our lives, only prolonging the blessings; perhaps forfeiting them as well. Strap yourself in and rest in the God of the universe. Rest in the mighty, righteous right hand of your loving Heavenly Father. I promise when you do you will awaken to a new child—happy, smiling, rested, and at peace in a land too beautiful for words.

> "Commit your works to the Lord and your plans will be established."
> Proverb 16:3

I have heard many people say that they have no regrets about the mistakes that they made in their lives because that is what has gotten them to be what they are today. I beg to differ. I would in a heartbeat change the mistakes I have made. They have caused me to miss blessings and experience increased heartache in my life. Had I trusted God for my future sooner, what greater rewards would I and would my family have received? Had I not committed such sins, how much grief and sorrow would I have spared others and myself? Had I stood for Christ, what other souls would I have encouraged to do the same? Regrets? Yes, definitely. But forgiveness? Most assuredly! Thank God we serve a God of forgiveness. Thank God He is a God of restoration. Thank

God He is a God of love. It is never too late to head for the city that He has prepared. Do not fear, blessed one, for He and His righteous right hand are near.

Reach out and take hold. Do not fear!

Made in the USA
Columbia, SC
27 September 2017